CD Included

Requires Windows 95 or Mac 8.6 or higher

Animal Antics

S0-AAZ-349

Creative Clip Art for Classroom and Home
Created and Designed by Dianne J. Hook

ISBN: 1-59441-487-4

Contents

Credits

Illustrator: Dianne J. Hook
Content Design and Project Director: Jennifer Weaver-Spencer
Editor: JulieAnna K. Kirsch
Cover Production: Pam Thayer

Animal Antics!

Clip Art Assembly Basics

Here are some suggestions to help you make flyers, announcements, or other projects using clip art from this book.

Tools

Putting together the right tools will help your project go more smoothly and look better in the end. A good **copy machine** is a must. It's worth the extra effort to make sure your school or copy shop has machines that make clean copies. You will also need a bottle of white **paper correction fluid**, a fine-tip **black marker** to combine designs and add your own art to the project, **rubber cement** to mount the design onto your paper during the layout stage, and **scissors** for cutting apart the designs you choose. Optional tools to help create a professional-looking project are a **nonreproducible blue pencil**, to make marks that will not show up on copies, a **proportion scale**, to help you determine the size of the reduction or enlargement necessary to fit your paper, and **blue grid paper** for laying out the project with straight lines.

Assembly Steps

1. Choose the design or designs you want to use for your project.

2. Copy the design once from the book so that you have a copy from which to work. This will keep you from having to cut apart your book.

3. Cut out the designs from your copy and lay them out on your paper. (Blue grid paper comes in handy.) A light table can also help with the layout of your page.

4. Next, make a copy of the designs and any text on the paper before adding any other hand-drawn illustrations. Drawing over the grid paper lines is difficult and generally doesn't turn out well.

5. Now you have a good idea of what your project is going to look like. Go ahead and add all the extra finishing touches. Small doodles, simple dots, or squares can really "warm up" the page and keep it from looking choppy.

6. Make final copies of your page.

Hints

- Keep a ¼-inch (0.64 cm) margin on all edges of your paper.
- If the edges of the cutout pieces are visible on your copies, lighten the copy machine one notch or use correction fluid on one copy. Then you can use it to make the final copies.
- Removable tape is great for creating layouts if you will be using the design more than once.

Clip Art Images on CD

Clip art images presented in black and white in this book are available in both black and white and color on the enclosed CD. The CD is Mac and PC compatible and requires an operating system of Windows 95/ Mac 8.6 or higher.

Have fun! You can become an artist and create wonderful projects for your class or home with the help of this book!

The Latest 'Moos'

Have You 'Herd'?

Farm Fun!

Oink!

Farm Animals
and
Their Babies

FEED
xxx

All About 'Ewe'!

Just for 'Ewe'!

Just 'Horsin' around'...

A Galloping Good Time!

A Day on the Farm

Giddy-Up !

My Favorite Animal is...

Don't Forget!

Wild About the ZOO

Zoo Fun!

Our Trip to the Zoo

'Grrrreat!'

A Roaring
Good Time!

Zoo
News

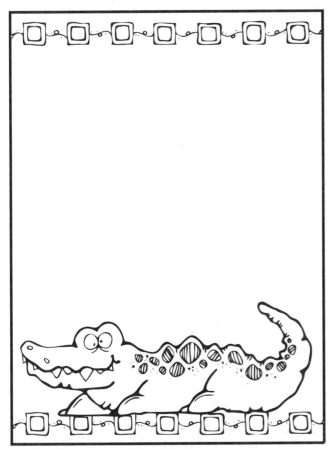

Go Wild!

Don't Forget
Your Signed
Permission Slip!

Field
Trip!

16

What's New at the Zoo?

Animals in the Woods

Moose on the Loose!

My BIG Ideas!

18

Squirrels

HOORAY
for YOU!

Great Thinking !

Have You Seen These Animals?

A walk in the woods

I can 'BEAR'-ly wait!

Woodland Creatures Border

21

Be
Wise

Look
WHOOO's
Doing
Great Work!

Woodland
Animals

Be WISE... and READ

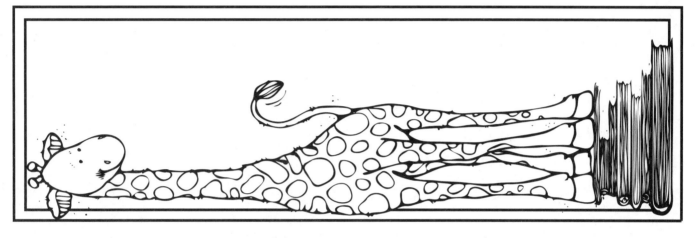

READ!

I 'CHEWS' to Read!

Critters

Cuddly Cats

I ♥ My Cat

Here Kitty Kitty!

Meow

MILK

Kitty

I Love My Pet!

Hooray!
Great!

Adopt a Pet!

I Love My Pet!

Ssssssmile!

My Best Friend!

'Bee' Yourself

'Bee' Respectful

'Bee' Nice

Bugs, Bugs, Everywhere!

"Look what I caught!"

32

**Butterflies
Make Me
Smile!**

It's a
Spring Thing!

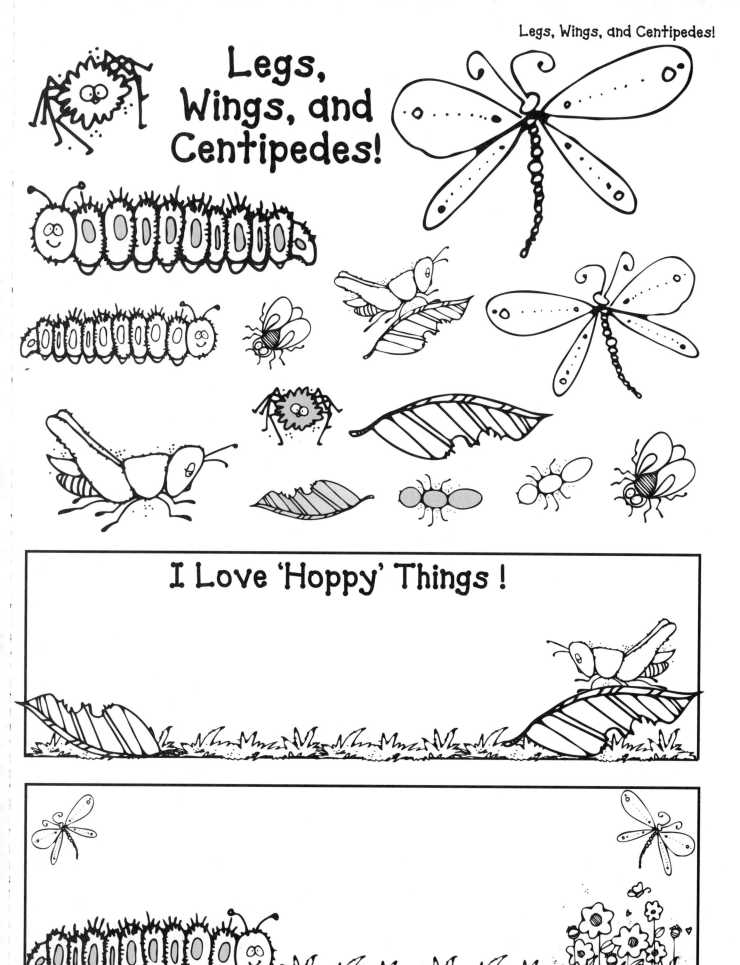

Legs, Wings, and Centipedes!

I Love 'Hoppy' Things!

34

A 'Flyer' to Parents

'Monkey-ing' Around!

Into the Jungle

Just 'MONKEY-ING' Around!

Time to Play!

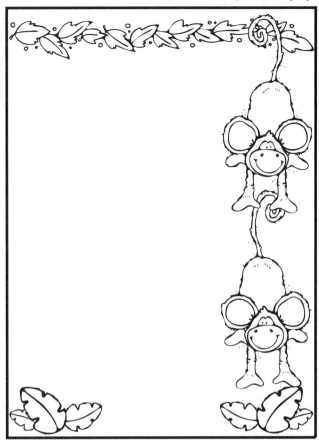

Jungle Animals

'HIPPO' Birthday to You!

Jungle Animals Border

Look who's Talking!

It's a jungle out there!

Where can you find me?

Sssuper Snakes!

Sssuper!

Our Classss is Besssst!

My SSSSummer Vacation...

Cool Animals!

Brrr! Polar Animals!

How do they
stay warm?

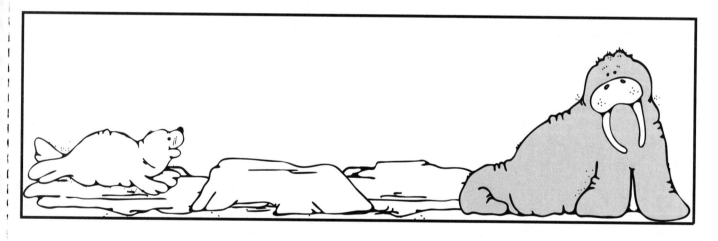

Under the Sea!

Into the Water

Sea Life

A Whale of a Tale!

Swimming Fun!

See
the
Sea

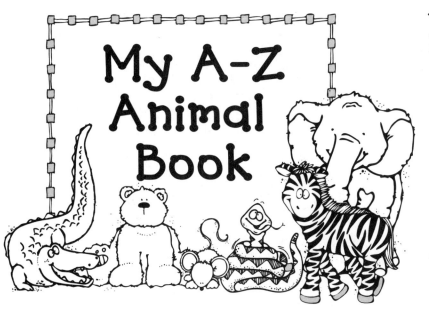

My A-Z Animal Book

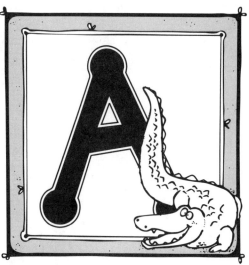

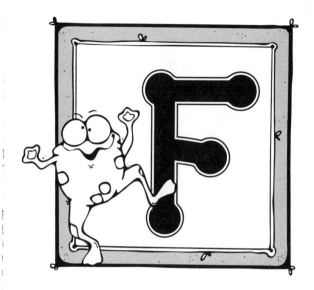

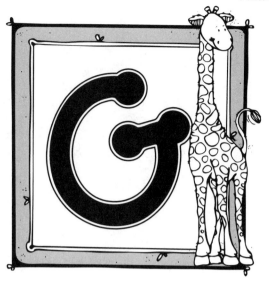

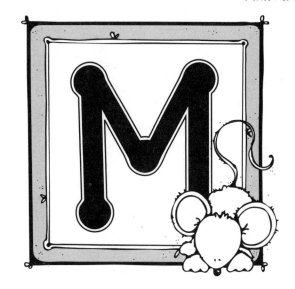

Animal Alphabet

A to Z

Animal Adventures!

Just 'Paws'ing

We're Having a Wild Time!

Teacher's Pet

It's a Zoo!

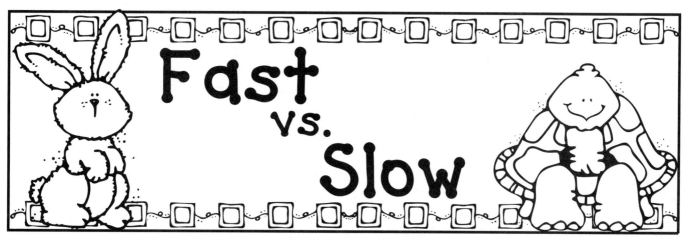

Fast vs. Slow

My Favorite Animal

The Latest 'MOOOOO-s'!

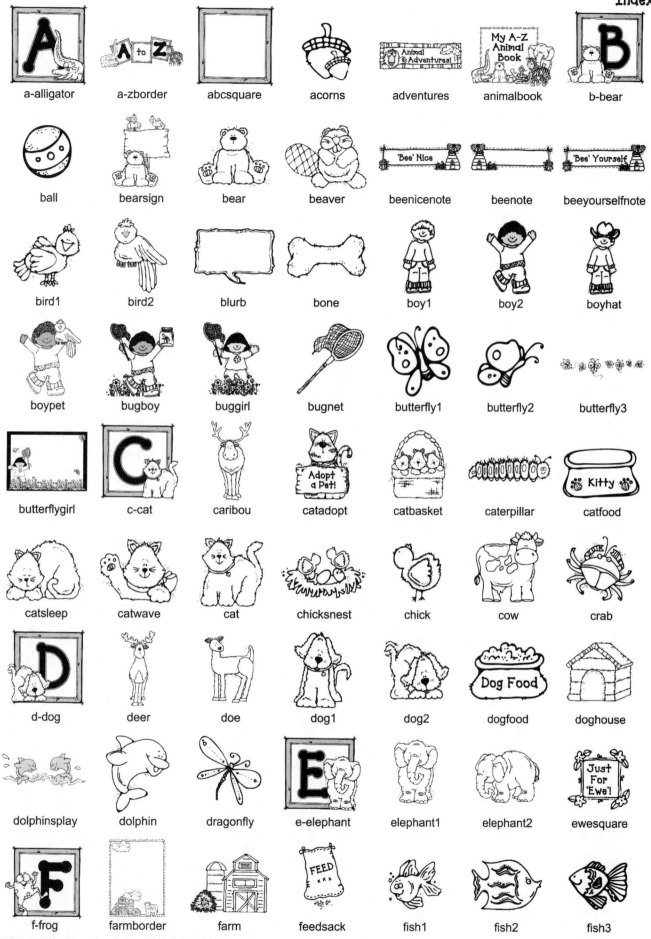

a-alligator   a-zborder   abcsquare   acorns   adventures   animalbook   b-bear

ball   bearsign   bear   beaver   beenicenote   beenote   beeyourselfnote

bird1   bird2   blurb   bone   boy1   boy2   boyhat

boypet   bugboy   buggirl   bugnet   butterfly1   butterfly2   butterfly3

butterflygirl   c-cat   caribou   catadopt   catbasket   caterpillar   catfood

catsleep   catwave   cat   chicksnest   chick   cow   crab

d-dog   deer   doe   dog1   dog2   dogfood   doghouse

dolphinsplay   dolphin   dragonfly   e-elephant   elephant1   elephant2   ewesquare

f-frog   farmborder   farm   feedsack   fish1   fish2   fish3

fishbowl   fly   g-giraffe   gatormark   gatornote   gator   giraffe1

giraffe2   girl1   girl2   girl3   girlpet   grasshopper1   grasshopper2

h-hippo   hamster1   hamster2   hamsterpeek   haystack   hen   hippo1

hippo2   hipponote   horse&kids   horse   i-iguana   iceblock   igloo

j-jellyfish   jar   jellyfish   jungleborder   jungletree   k-kangaroo   kangaroo&joey

koala   l-lion   ladybugborder   ladybugflyer   ladybugnote   ladybug   leaf

lioness   lionnote   lionsign   lion   m-mouse   monkey1   monkey2

monkeynote   monkeysign   mooseframe   moosemark   moose   moostopper   moomark

mountains   mouse   myfavorite   n-newt   o-octopus   octopus   opossum

ostrich	owlmark	owl	p-penguin	parrot	pawsing	paws
penguin1	penguin2	penguinmark	penguinpage	petborder	pigborder	pig
pinecone	polarbear	porcupine	q-quail	quiltheart	r-racoon	rabbit1
rabbit2	racoon	rooster	s-snake	seaborder	seahorse	sealbaby
seal	seaplant	seaturtle	shark	sheepborder	sheep	shell1
shell2	shell3	shell4	skunk	snakenote	snake	snowball
snowsign	spider	squirrel1	squirrel2	stick	t-turtle	tigernote
tigertiny	tiger	toad	toucan	tree	turtle1	turtle2
turtlenote	twig	u-unicorn	v-vulture	w-walrus	walrusice	walrusmark

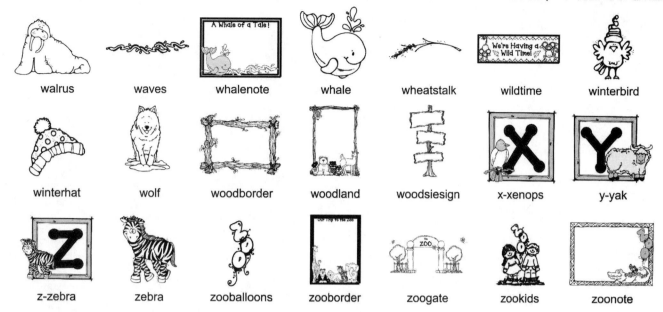

walrus	waves	whalenote	whale	wheatstalk	wildtime	winterbird
winterhat	wolf	woodborder	woodland	woodsiesign	x-xenops	y-yak
z-zebra	zebra	zooballoons	zooborder	zoogate	zookids	zoonote

zoomark

Please note that all the images in this book are not contained on the CD.

Clip Art Information: DJ Inkers Cut & Copy for Computer CDs contain clip art in both black and white and color. The clip art is not a program. It is a collection of art images to be used in a host program. The Windows CDs are formatted with .wmf file types. Macintosh CDs are formatted with .eps and .tiff file types. A host program that supports these file types is required. Recommended host programs for Windows include Print Shop, Print Master, or MS Publisher. Recommended programs for Macintosh include Appleworks or Claris.

Inserting Clip Art into a Host Program: Open a blank document. Click on *Insert > Clip Art > From File*, and select your "c:" drive. Double-click on the DJ Inkers folder, and double-click on the appropriate CD folder (ex. Kidillywinks). Double-click on *Vector*. You will now be viewing all the different images. Click on an image, and select *Insert*. This will insert the image into your document. These instructions can be applied to different host programs, although there may be some variation in the words used. For example, it may say *Import* or *Add* instead of *Insert*.

For further instructions or information, please visit our website, www.djinkers.com. Go to the *Tips & Ideas* section, and click on the *Frequently Asked Questions* link.